A CONSTITUTIONAL LAWSUIT IN FEDERAL COURT.

(DYFS)DCPP STATE WORKER(s) HELD ACCOUNTABLE PURSUANT TO SECTION 1983;85;86 and various additional claim(s)

as news media validate…

Author:

WOMEN 4 JUSTICE PUBLISHING N.Y.C. in association with:

T.A.N. (Take ACTION NETWORK)for the truly innocent.

Ext.806

Chapter I-

S*he was up against all odds. Until 1 day she realize her potential in learning and studying aggressively, tirelessly the law, to make it her passion, 24hrs.a day where all else had to take a back seat to her* **mission.**

She modeled, actress auditions in nyc for television/movie/soaps auditions since a pre-teen girl and a songstress, hip hop lyricist,along with loving her nice suburban life. She was on her way to make her complete album in N.Y.C.

until 1 day, a 4th of july visit court-ordered, and those of such jealousy, hatred, and a troublesome life of all others and an agency for the state per employee interrupted her good life, turned it upside down and as a result her life trajectory has changed into a law-motivational-mindset, knowing more law than any attorney to cross her path, for which,

 coast to coast the author is being lauded by such lawyer(s)who at first, said she couldn't do it.

Her winning suit for her family pro-se was filed, and the rest is history. *Her life however, will never be the same again, but shall continue to be a "Voice to those who are voiceless."*

Chapter II-

Inspiring a NATION.

No one would get in the way of her clear mission of developing her own blueprint, and business org., et.al., that would assist others,

for educational general purposes only guide a helpful pro-se on winning @ *the same level* she has on her own without a lawyer when time is running out to sue known as PRO-SE(self file)a state employee for various torts, claims, violations against such party of innocence.

Her mission to:

- ➤ Become her own lawyer, detective during such time of her fighting tirelessly over 10 yrs, for JUSTICE as some experts call it FINAL JUSTICE in the U.S.DISTRICT FEDERAL COURT.

- ➤ Become her own investigator in order to properly and timely discern,demonstrate,and win against a state agency employee as her daughter's life depend on it along with all three of their future.
- ➤ Become a civil rights parental advocate, grandparent,child activist, law student, and an empowerment speaker to motivate EDUCATE, ENCOURAGE + teach those violated by a state employee, when such person or person(s)think it is hopeless, to hold 1 accountable just because an O.S.A.(old school attorney) do NOT care about one's family or right to sue..

Don't give up when you're in the right.

The nation's first:

Women 4 JUSTICE Publishing thank you all for reading our

docu-series, volume 1 through 15. To take part in such screenplay currently in development, call the help/hotline-directly office line for owner/author founder.

Thank you.

Chapter III-

Prior to the author's publicized-lawsuit pro-se, there were other injuries forced upon America's most innocent. The children. Many right out of New Jersey.

1 billion dollar reform in N.J. was taking place while multiple children were being:

- STARVED TO NEAR-DEATH AND OR STARVED TO DEATH...
- MALTREATMENT.
- MISTREATMENT.

- RAPED.
- SEXUALLY ABUSED.
- MOLESTATION
- OVERLY MEDICATED
- DRUGGED/PSYCHO-TROPIC MEDICATION HARM.
- EDUCATIONAL NEGLECT(once removed from loving home)
- MEDICAL DENTAL NEGLECT(once removed from the home)
- DEATH UNDER STATE SUPERVISION AND CARE.
- LOST IN THE SYSTEM.

We,

The hard-working astute 1 of a kind ctr., over @

WOMEN 4 JUSTICE PUBLISHING N.Y.C. share some with you and also information valid from the owner's own most warranted suit. We thank you for reading our docu-series, now being made into a 2017-2018 screenplay. Help line available 24hrs.a day.

Chapter IV-

An unprecedented level of NJ state funding to re-invent NJ troubled agency system of "DCF DYFS DCPP" of protecting such neglected/abused children was unveiled early 2000's throughout the past decade, as the state and quoting such history records, news media reports," to end not a day or a month or two, but an entire DECADE, actually **DECADES**(plural) of mis-management at the state's child protection services agency. $125 MILLION within the coming year to revamp the "troubled Division Youth Families Services, assailed for the past 12 or 13 months or so, over a series, as news validae, a series of

HIGH-PROFILE **DYFS RELATED** TRAGEDIES, that clearly

did NOT have to happen.

Admissions from such agency, and the governor at the time admit how

"we have failed."

Failed the children for far too long as news articles cite. Under the current system of DCF, investigators,casework state employees, are not investigating the way they are supposed to,news report cite, and are not doing it "quick enough, officials have cited."

Chapter V-

Excerpt from such news media article involving such troubling agency DCP&P(NJ DYFS,DCF,CPS)where such state worker's and or governor at the time admit that:

One of the fundamental problems of this system has been that caseloads were simply too high. "That leads to bad decision making, and failures in the system.

Under NJ reform(involving Federal Court Watch)involving 1 billion dollar reform:

- ➢ Child protection workers and permanency workers have less cases.

- ➢ Child protection workers would specialize in investigations of child abuse and neglect, receive special forensic training and would be limited to a caseload of eight new investigations per month.

- ➢ Permanency workers would provide the ongoing services to children and families and have a maximum caseload of 15 families or 10 children in out of home placement.

➤ The people in New Jersey have been appalled by the horrific abuse and neglect documented in stories about children under the auspices of DYFS now refer to as the D.C.P.P. (DCF) but not much has changed since the state caseworker's are supposed to be "doing their job and protecting the lives of children whom are placed under their supervision."

➤ Regardless of what a state employee shall inform you and attempt to avoid being sued, to avoid such liability, by citing, "It's not our responsibility and or how they can't be blamed for whatever bad happens to such child, it is indeed the state employees fault, the state agency employees onus to ensure the safety of such children as long as they are under state supervision and care…*No way around it.*

Chapter V-

DCPP authority and interest in protecting children does not allow such (confidential) and or a multitude of faceless allegations to override the clearly-established privacy rights of such American N.J. citizens and moreover,

the rights to be free from **warrantless searches** under our State *and* Federal Constitutions. U.S.Const., amend. IV, XIV, N.J.Const., arts. 1, 7, 10; New Jersey Civil Rights Act, N.J.S.A. 10:6-2(c)

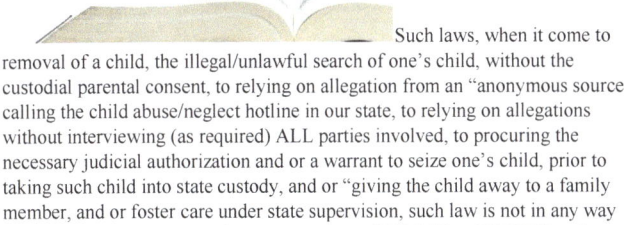 Such laws, when it come to removal of a child, the illegal/unlawful search of one's child, without the custodial parental consent, to relying on allegation from an "anonymous source calling the child abuse/neglect hotline in our state, to relying on allegations without interviewing (as required) ALL parties involved, to procuring the necessary judicial authorization and or a warrant to seize one's child, prior to taking such child into state custody, and or "giving the child away to a family member, and or foster care under state supervision, such law is not in any way unclear, no matter how much a state employee CHOOSE to IGNORE such.

The current **$50million** *dollar in damages suit that has won without (a lawyer)was able to move forward, at the pro-se level,* approved *by federal court, as the discussion in this book on other publicized cases, is proof that not much has changed within the* **"system."**

The author and her family has underscore such and that has been a huge help to others, who are still suffering from being clearly mistreated, abused by their own caseworker, even 1 caseworker calling a child under 18 under her supervision and care nothing but a "pathological liar."

Some form of DCF collusion is clear to many, involving the author's warranted civil rights lawsuit. Author, at jury trial for civil right damages during the latter part of 2017 if not reasonably settled, shall be able to show the consciousness of such wrongdoing, insofar as multiple employees at the state **child protection agency.**

Such wrongful and the continual hinderance of such substantial information relating to her daughter's care and well-being when unlawfully removed from her loving custody, has underlay her 24hours a day to ensure the truth is revealed insofar as what the caseworker **KNEW, what the caseworker had done, and who did what, when where,and who all know, as experts agree that**

case deserve a jury trial to flush out the truth and to have a jury assess it all and for liability to be hereto, properly attached for years of wrongful act(s)and gross-negligence on behalf of the state and or their individual employees.

What caseworker would ever refer to a child as a liar, let alone and we are now quoting a dcf employee for the state as withheld reports prove, and part of our lawsuit winning, a caseworker cites, "pathological liar" about an innocent and severely abused(under state supervision) child, while knowingly willfully with malice lie to the court by making it appear as if she is doing her job, and protecting such child,and attempting to reunify child with parent.

Such parties reading suit and learning about this is citing to the mom, how the state employee must have ICE in her veins to call a child that who has been clearly:

- ➢ *Wrongfully removed.*

- ➢ Unlawfully/Continually detained, in state custody and as a result has suffered grave abuse/serious injuries in a foster care system where she never belong and this was again everyone to all our many readers, KNOWN to the caseworker, as the child rights, while being violated, you're having a caseworker refer to a innocent helpless severely injured child as a pathological liar.

Naturally...

This was not shared with the union county family superior court judge.

Neither were a voluminous amount of other shocking records/files all withheld, now discovered, in support of such lawsuit for damages.

This demonstrate a caseworker and or worker's who clearly do not have the **BEST interest** of the child on their mind,and has worked hard to do anything but, as the record to a jury of their peers will demonstrate in favor of the child and her loving parent.

Depraved indifference, when the child is clearly at risk, and or hungry (children being forbidden to have food) has been featured in the news as well in other winning lawsuits for such inhumane treatment, and also was exerted by the child to the author,her mother, during conversations after she was reunited with mom. Yet, a caseworker state employee J.S., always would make it appear and knowingly lying that the child was doing fine and that there was no risk to her whatsoever, as already covered in several other authored books now available.

One cold winter's day, the author took a drive to the more seedy-part of her beloved state of New Jersey to see a house/area where a little boy her child age was brutally abused,neglected leading to him going to heaven early premise on the same agency sloppy careless cruel and imcompetent neglect of such beautiful little boy for so long, as news reports covered such story for years.

Author drove to Newark aka Brick City, in N.J.

She bought a single rose and a card and placed it down to where Faheem was last found.

She had to see for herself a make shift memorial for a beautiful little boy, her daughter's age, who, at only seven years young was now RIP too early in heaven premise on DCF.Such tragedy happened the same exact year as her daughter(then only 10 and 7) had been legally kidnapped as experts call it and others nationally.

Chapter VII-

Sweet little boy by the beautiful name of "Faheem."

A beautiful little boy residing in a not so great part of NJ where crime runs rampant, is clearly in need of city-reform itself, sweet little boy,pure,innocent who was supposed to be loved, playing with his toys at Christmas, or going on an Easter egg hunt, or receiving a little box of chocolate candy for Valentine's day, or enjoying a fire truck,or a toy police car, or blue clues on Nickelodeon, but rather was forcibly tied up in a basement and later found dead.

FAHEEM WILLIAMS,

Of Newark, dead while his twin brother lived and another brother. As she sat outside his house of horrors, the author drop a tear or two while she watch as media was all over the story and conducting interviews with a neighbor next door to the make-shift memorial at Faheem's last place he was seen alive and found dead. A name I personally shall never forget.

The author later learned how the new jersey child protection services agency DCF had closed his family's case out prematurely. May he RIP.

Caseworker, on such case clearly dropped the ball and do not care, because, as all agree,

"THIS WAS **NOT** THEIR CHILD/AND OR FAMILY MEMBER."

These workers as experts and others agree, should have been locked up, as in other states where caseworker's do get charged accordingly,booked,arraigned when you're either:

- Lying under oath to a material fact
- Engaging in perjury knowingly,willfully,deliberately et.al.,
- Misconduct.
- Malice.

Chapter VIII-

Another high profile shocking the conscience case involving such worker's in NJ, are of four young boys adopted by a troubled abusive family in south jersey.

The Jackson boys, suffering years of malnutrition. Yet DYFS said, "We had visited the boys."

Dozens of such children were either neglected severely and or abused so badly, for years under "state care and supervision of DYFS, whose actual plight of such child was only revealed, because of a great org., by the name of CHILDREN RIGHTS INC;

Had pried open the complete DCPP(dyfs,dcf) file

and let it all come to light as to what was really going on,

with these assigned supervisors,casework employees for the state in the aforesaid mention shocking the conscience cases.

When a JURY of the author's peers in the U.S.District Federal Ct.,

any day now, begin to examine, go over such facts presented properly to the court for damages, (as experts agree) when a **jury** hear from also the loving family who suffered so gravely, and what happened to 2 little suburban happy little healthy girls, (author daughter's) and how the worker as in the prior cases, allowed them to extreme-suffer, and knew and yet did nothing to preclude,nothing to reunite

(AS REQUIRED in the home with mom) the jury will do what is right experts are predicting after years of waiting for FINAL justice involving such loving innocent once happy family.

Such jury shall hear it all and shall shock the conscience as case law wholly support,

shall shock the conscience.

Now, not all are able to as experts agree PROVE such shocking the conscience and or liability,

but at least in the author meritorious suit she will be able to, as the file(s)not seen for SEVERAL YEARS, finally are seen and support wholly what has already been expounded in our warranted docu-series for Shocking the Conscience and "I Swear, To Tell A Lie" along with ALLEGATION, THE WEEKEND VISIT, PART I,

along with other books now available, for which is being made, as we speak into a 2 to 4 hour television and or documentary series, as we speak,throughout 2017-and all of 2018.)So, stay tuned everyone.

Just **remember**, as all books shall remind everyone worldwide, that the assigned worker in the author's $50MILLION in damages suit had for some time, not only mislead the mother,on her child's condition, but mislead the superior union county courthouse(family court) in all subsequent hearings, and mislead the judge adjudicating on whether or not to return the child to her mother, and or to have un-fettered access as she is entitle to, relating to her own daughter's while custody was being considered, along with her younger sister and knowingly with malice, intentionally for some time would mislead at each, turn the judge **about the overall** nature of her(dcf caseworker) communications, with hospitals,to conversations and knowledge of risk,relating to the abusive step-mother in the home of the father, a troubled drug addict alcoholic & a convicted felon who serve time in jail/prison, for such crimes, NOT fit at ANY TIME he had custody to be around the girls let alone attempt to raise both girls at 10 and 7 years old through the teenage child years.

Chapter IX

As cited above, in the JACKSON BOYS(SOUTH JERSEY case)

News reports and research cites how the DYFS did not know at any time just about how the boys, were "receiving medical check-ups and also dental et.al., in school." A reporter ask the agency, "How will this change, with the NEW DYFS agency system to PREVENT such next time, when a child under state supervision is involved?"

Their response?

We are expanding **the six-month case review** where a case reviewer will sit with the worker, the foster family, the child if the child is of school age & the entire BIRTH BIOLOGICAL family,

if they are still involved and rights have **not** been terminated.

Every six months, there will be a review that includes:

- **medical records.**
- **the educational records**.

And if a judge is involved, shall be reported to the judge overseeing such family superior court case/hearings et.al.,

Now...

To all our readers...

This, did not happen (in violation of the author family now suing for damages.

This never happened.

The review period is crucial and mandatory.

It's supposedly to see how well the child is doing in state care and under state supervision, while out of parent home.

A review is crucial, to see if the goals are being met, and if the child and or children are progressing, as the news and dyfs own handbook/policy requires.

NJ FAMILY TEAM MEETINGS ARE SUPPOSED TO OCCUR WITH ALL FAMILY MEMBERS INVOLVED.

(Not just 1 parent.) Such family team meetings are to discuss each and every IMPORTANT DECISION, related to the child "if you're having a case that is open with NJ DCPP.

As the governor/and or the agency spokesman cites, "We no longer will be operating in a vacuum, and or we don't want our caseworker's any longer, making such decisions relating to the child, in a vacuum. We will bring together, not only the state employee(caseworker) but a teacher, or a family member might want an "aunt" there at the F.T.M,

and or a grandmother, on either side of the family, and if a child let's say "needed to be removed, there will be then a discussion amongst ALL PARTIES involved, about whom the child should stay with."

[End Quote.]

The article featured in the news for years everyone,

so be sure to look it up or call our help/hotline consulting et.al., any time 24hrs.a day.

This was again not the case with the author, who has not, at any time, for over and almost 8 years, sat in with a dyfs caseworker, nor informed there was a F.T.M taking place in violation of her right,as the children.

Such lawsuit on the wrongful act(s)involving such troubled caseworker's are not in any way unclear and is public.

Chapter X-

To substantiate and or not substantiate/establish abuse.

When you're a state employee (dcf employee) such "confidential" information allegedly gathered, in order to make a finding of either abuse and or neglect, risk of harm et.al., and maintain such permanent file involving one's family, without the ability for

a parent to be allowed to seek,

a Due-Process Review involving such caseworker's determination,

is a violation.

IN VIOLATION OF CLEAR LAW(CONSTITUTION OF NJ)

When DYFS (DCP&P) has such probable cause everyone, to conduct such search involving one's child, your home et.al., there is a mechanism to procure such access DYFS has probable cause to conduct a search there is a mechanism to obtain access to a residence, to your child, and then the worker present such to the court in many cases(some made public for years) pursuant to N.J.S.A. 9:6-8.

However,

DYFS(dcpp) when there is NO IMMINENT DANGER and or what is known as EXIGENT CIRCUMSTANCES, relating to your house/and or child,

The state agency employees must procure such warrant or a judicial approval,authorization to remove our children, from our primary legal residential care.

It's not that prevalent though that the worker takes the time to adhere to such law, as a state official,public employee, state employee, by adhering to such law by the procurement of a judicial approved court order first.

It is common actually the worker engage in such practice prior to the actual "SEARCH and SEIZURE OF ONE'S CHILD, without the necessary required court order, and or warrant, as such investigatory actions/removal of your child happens usually in violation of one's constitutional right,for which shall continue to, as experts agree result in lawsuits across the nation and our state, tri-state area and shall, as a result end up ***on extreme*** cases like the author, lead to a child, being found(After removal) either harmed,seriously injured,raped,sexually abused, hospitalized,and or bullied,overly medicated, or DEAD.

DCF/DCPP state employees(not all but many the author have met, and prior forcibly had to deal with, as other cases show when Child Protection Services NJ employees,as in other states, demand such access to one's home and or child, it usually will do so, under such intimidating circumstances, placing a high-level of fear in such parent,grandparent at the time of DCF involvement. Such actions by the caseworker,supervisor assigned, *does not*, as lawyer expertise in such field,and experts all agree with the author that such does not comply with our well-established citizen protections under the Constitution of the State of New Jersey and does so in violation of the law.

Chapter XI

FACTS TAKEN FROM OWNER'S PUBLICIZED MERITORIOUS SUIT:

A NJ DCP&P(dyfs,dcf)employee cites, "Mom's false allegations/all are BOGUS."

Such statement said by a defendant, newly discovered through discovery prove that at the time such shocking statement was said, by a defendant now being sued, it turns out that:

1. Allegations against a crack-fein/alcoholic/heroine inject/user was true.
2. Allegations against a troubled abusive/drunk of a step-parent was true.
3. Allegations such daughter of the author was at staid risk for not days but years on end, were all 100% accurate, for which the caseworker again earlier was citing to others, "Pathlogical liar mom and her child."

Caseworker also cite that ALL the injuries, severely gruesome, at the time the child was living under state supervision, were *the fault of* the daughter for being and we quote, "A bad child,and by not listening to her dad?" A caseworker who knew, at the time the child was clearly at staid risk,blame the child.

Reports (supporting lawsuit for damages for over/almost a decade by state worker include such facts/evidence but not limited to:

➢ Hindered the fact that multiple employees for the nj union county DYFS feign, the fact pix did indeed exist that would've so easily cleared such parent and the girls and parent would have never been injured almost 15 years now.

➢ Hindered the fact the *photographs* taken during such investigation (without mom knowledge)caseworker even told the higher Court of Appeals, "dyfs worker had no knowledge of any photographs taken to support mom version of the fact that no injuries consistent with abuse had even existed."

➢ Yet, the mother had discovered such shocker along with her amazing (then custody lawyer) of bergen county, nj, who fought long and fought hard for her after other five lawyers failed her(exept Karin R.White)

> *Mr. Jonathan D. Gordon Esq, and mom learned through a tip, there was existing photographs* depicting her girls were at NOT at any risk at all. Such fact(s) were also known to nj cps agency DYFS, DCF.

The 4th- 14th amendment claim is not in any way unclear and shall be soon god-willing won as all experts are predicting from coast-to-coast.

1. The laws were clearly-established for the children during such time for years, involving the fourth/fourteenth amendment, the right to :
   A.) Not be deprived of their right to go HOME.

   B.) Not to be deprived their own mother.

   C.) Not to be deprived of the right to live with their parent and to be raised with a drug-free, good loving doting mother in a drug-free home.

   D.) The right to be free from UNREASONABLE SEARCHES.

   E.) The right to be free from an UNLAWFUL, continual seizure.

Hence, her injured family timely filed pro-se (without a lawyer self file litigant)

$50MILLION DOLLAR SUIT for untold damages, multiple documented years worth of serious injuries, countless number of civil right and constitutional right violations et.al, for almost a decade strong, when **all the state agency employees had to do was adhere to policy.**

Couldn't do it.

The agency state employees assigned to such publicly profile case just couldn't do it… This is fact. No opinion, no bald assertion(s) just fact.

Any other caring and good social worker would have not eNgage in such pattern of clear flagrant gross-negligent ILLEGAL acts unbecoming to a state employee."

Hence, as a result mom and girls suffered as all experts worldwide agree immensely, untold damages for years and years to come everyone.

1-929-277-7848

Ext. 806

DYFS employees at the Union County Local office willfully, recklessly,or intentionally for almost a decade shocking the conscience of all worldwide, from lawyers, police, to experts,to our readers nationwide, CPS knew and or acted with clear recklessness for some time, when they were falsely accusing such loving parent, hiding the daughter's at risk situation(once removed) quite well for several years, breaking the law while doing so,

kept the girls at each turn away from mom, without ever making a necessary by law, finding of abuse,imminent danger,exigent circumstance, neglect, serious physical injury; and or proving 'on the day in question, the loving parent was a risk to the child; as sued (properly)for 14th Amendment violation,

the interviewing of her girls without a primary residential parent consent at the time, to suing for the additional claim(s)of emotional distress for almost eight years,for holding her 2 girls without such cause; fabricating years on end; fabricating evidence and for such improper training of its' DCF employee(s)assigned to this most tragic case.

Additionally, supporting punitive damage(s) et.al, as experts agree:

-Hindered the fact the loving parent, our founder:

-**After** child was sadly illegally/unlawfully/unconstitutionally detained,

the girls suffered horrific torture for years at each level."

State agency, and or its individual cps employees clearly knew.

At least 1/2 dozen minimum to a dozen knew at one time or another over eight years yet withheld such shocking fact(s)insofar as but not limited to one child was not even at the home of the ex spouse as cps sworn-in under oath, lieing for years saying she was and how "well"she was doing living with her father, his new wife. Child was hence shockingly "_missing_."

DCPP,DYFS has now lost the child, while mom is still being

>Barred from seeing her.

>Intentionally mis-informed her girls, both were doing well, under "state" supervision and there is no risk to either.

Another report withheld by these specified liable dyfs employees prove that and have stated how DYFS knew that the mother (author) had a legal right to "bring the child home as said by another caseworker, working under the supervision of a child protection services(DYFS) supervisor who himself, refer to as C.N.,

also knew such factual information, but yet NO ONE turned over such relevant credible evidence, prior to a lengthy un-warranted farce of prosecution fact find hearing, a trial against this now injured(severely)for years loving parent, turn law student pursuing for a law degree in due course in California + East coast.

She has seen what has happen in all states mentioned, where her family are living,nieces,nephews,siblings to parents,her family across state to local,and she will pass the bar exam for other innocent GOOD souls to NOT have to suffer by "not being able to win against CPS, as she now has after almost 14 yrs of suffering herself, **UNCONSTITUTIONAL**.

News report verified, the founder of such incredible network,biz.org, et.al., the author multi-million dollar suit for damages pursuant to SECTION 1983,85 et.al., has won the significant right to move forward, as per discovery has now been implemented, along with summary judgement phase, for which we have no doubt, that FINAL justice is near, as experts agree, when reviewing and following publicly such meritorious and much needed civil rights lawsuit.

3rd District....

unlike incompetent bias state court,at least in this case, the FEDERAL court,has done what was warranted, and that is to give the family injured back a modicum of justice long over since early 2000's, to the late 2000's., the news verified suit was filed pursuant to U.S.C.A. Title 42 Section 1983 AND conspired act against caseworkers, employees for the Department of Child Protection & Permanency prior DYFS, and still refer to also as DCF.

She filed it all on her own without a lawyer. (Not for the lack of trying everyone.She called 118+ lawyers coast-to-coast,but not one(at the *initial* filing suit phase)not one lawyer "caring or astute to file."

It sure didn't stop her none, hence the rest is history proving you **CAN** sue for per injury associated with DCF.

The owner of the FIRST **NATIONWIDE** NETWORK of its kind, along with her daughters and her family,banned together, and made sure that as a team, a loving family, with GOD along their side, the **FACTS** finally after so long will reach a "fair" **and impartial non-bias** FAIR judge for consideration in the U.S. District Federal Court.

Such lawsuit consist of various torts, state common law/and additionally federal claim(s) and other staid numerous cited claims associated with the clear destruction of a parent/child right to remain home and free from infringement of one's rights, under the United States Constitution and won.

Good luck when you're suing and holding accountable a state employee for civil right damages everyone. It can be done, so don't think it can't, without or with attorney.

Ask for ext. 806 after help form is implemented.

Remember:

 *It is not the lies, invoke by a state attorney, it is not the voice the yells loudest in the courtroom by **providing** such fraudulent and **mischaracterization** (deliberate/intentional et.al.)*

but what shall prevail, at the end of the day when all is said and done premise on a reasonable jury, and or trier of fact, is our American U.S.Constitution,

when you're suing for such damages a state employee, with competent,

credible evidence**, a** set of fact(s)that shall be the **ultimate** victory of those **truly** injured/violation by a DCF employee,**CPS.**

TO BE CONTINUED.

Entire volume one throughout fifteen are now featured and available at Barnes & Nobles U.K., U.S.A., Amazon, Books-A-Million et.al., and nationwide retailers:

I SWEAR TO TELL **A LIE**, YOUR HONOR.

THE NUTS & BOLTS, WHILE SUING A STATE EMPLOYEE PRO-SE.

SUING CHILD PROTECTION SERVICES STATE EMPLOYEE BY DEADLINE. (PRO-SE)WITHOUT A LAWYER.

MOMMIE, MOMMIE, CAN I GO HOME NOW?

<u>**A CASEWORKER**</u> ENGAGE IN THE UNTHINKABLE, IS HELD <u>ACCOUNTABLE</u> IN UNITED STATES FEDERAL DISTRICT COURT.

#ALLEGATION

WHEN A LAWYER DO NOT REPRESENT A CLIENT VIOLATED BY A STATE EMPLOYEE, FOR DAMAGES, LEARN AND FILE PRO-SE."

A LEGAL **KIDNAPPING** LEADS TO A **$50MILLION** DOLLAR MERITORIOUS FEDERAL CIVIL RIGHTS.

A DAY IN THE LIFE OF <u>**A PERJURED**</u> CASEWORKER @ DCFS.

A CONSTITUTIONAL RIGHT LAWSUIT.

THE WEEKEND VISIT.(PART I)

+

SHE <u>NEVER</u> GAVE UP . . .

(She never gave up is a true account of an ordinary suburban happy go luck ymom who had to become her own detective/lawyer experts agree to find the truth against DCPP,several state employees who assume they would get away with engaging in the unthinkable relating to such American Child and her loving mother. . .

Getting closer, to prove such CPS,DCF fraud upon/on the court, and such malice, conspired act, more than any other known parent, to prove such caseworker fraud on the court, perjury to a material fact, and downright malfeasance,to win family suit….and hold each and every state employee accountable without a lawyer.

Inspiration for many who are truly violated by a state employee.

Author now focus on the procurement of her Law Degree, in California, and East coast.

Other books now available, from the author including, but not limited to:

A DCF FORMER VICTIM to a Civil Rights ACTION Advocate +
LAW STUDENT PROCURING JURIS DOCTORAL (LAW DEGREE)

WOMEN 4 JUSTICE PUBLISHING N.Y.C.

INQUIRIES, MEDIA NEWS, BOOKINGS, INTERVIEWS, EXPERT INPUT FOR **AUTHOR'S FILM DOCUMENTARY BY:**

BOSS/AUTHOR/OWNER...

FILM ENTITLED:

Mommie, mommie...

(CAN I GO HOME NOW?)

SHOCKING THE CONSCIENCE.

Her VISION is not in any way unclear... *SCREENPLAY PREVIEW COMING SOON DURING THE YEAR OF 2017-2018.*

#**OUR RIGHTS DO MATTER** ...

EXT. 920

www.ingramcontent.com/pod-product-compliance
Lightning Source LLC
Chambersburg PA
CBHW041121180526
45172CB00001B/369